I CANT

YOU CAN GET THE ESSENCE
YOU CAN GET THE ENERGY
YOU CAN GET THE IMPOSSIBLE

A MANUAL FOR HAPPINESS

Written by **FRANK BASTOW**

Illustrated by **DAVID WATTS**

I'd like to dedicate this book to my Wife, kids, family and friends. Without whom.... I wouldn't need this f***ing book!

DONT BE A CANT

Introduction

Why this book ?

Every day and in every way I get up and try my hardest not to be a complete and utter CANT.

Some days it's easy; other days let's just say I find it quite challenging.

I don't believe anyone ever really wants to be a CANT. However, I'm still shocked and upset at the amount of time and energy I see people use in explaining, arguing and trying to prove why they are complete and utter CANTS.

So I thought I would have the audacity to share some ideas that might stop all of us doing stupid stuff.

Please note...

Everything in this book is bought, borrowed or stolen. It's full of clichés, too, but clichés are often one of the easiest ways to help understanding or make a point.

This book may very well make you rich, famous and more attractive to the opposite (or same) sex. But if it doesn't and you can only acquire its essence, life will become a lot easier and almost certainly a lot happier.

Happiness, like the Meaning of Life, God or any Stephen Hawking book, is a difficult concept to grasp. Hopefully this book will help you achieve your own version of happiness.

And one last thing; ideas are worthless unless they are turned into reality and acted upon.

I do hope you enjoy stumbling through my un-muddied mind ;)

How this book works

3 SIMPLE RULES

1 YOU CAN GET THE ESSENCE Get the best out of this life.

2 YOU CAN GET THE IMPOSSIBLE Get what you want from this life.

3 YOU CAN GET THE ENERGY Get the energy you need out of this life.

THEN

WHENEVER YOU GET A "GREAT IDEA", STOP.

GO TO THE END OF THIS BOOK, AND WRITE IT DOWN UNDER "EUREKA MOMENTS".

ALSO, AT THE END OF EACH CHAPTER ARE "NEXT STEPS" YOU CAN JOT DOWN (AND THINK BIG…), AND YOU CAN COMMIT TO THEM AT THE END IF THEY STILL EXCITE YOU.

THEY EVEN HAVE TICK BOXES FOR WHEN YOU'VE ACHIEVED THEM.

'I WANNA TELL YOU A STORY'

Stories are a great way to explain a point, and the more ridiculous the better. I have taken stories that have had a profound impact upon my life's journey and my own life experiences and included them here - whether good, bad or indifferent.

So, here is one of the stories to show how you CAN or CANT choose to get value out of this book.

The Magic Trick

I now spend part of my working life investing in energetic entrepreneurs, each looking for support in their special endeavour. It's really important that I work with people who are aligned with me, so how I identify them is to show them a 'magic trick'. Not a card trick, but a Personal or Business tool that will change their life for the better, IMHO. They normally freak out and say, "Tell me how you do that?"

I explain the trick or tool, and one of two things happens.

EITHER

80% of people look at me, and I can see the questions and excuses dancing all over their face. After being so excited they say they've worked out that they have to go down to the 'magic shop', buy the trick, practice for weeks perfecting it and the worst bit, have to perform it in public.

But they then say, "Yeah I kind of worked that out. But I kinda …… Blah Blah Blah!" These are the CANTS!!!!

OR

20% of people look at me and say, "You mean all I have to do is go to the 'magic shop', buy the trick, practice and perform it and I'll get all these results?" I love these people – they're the CANS !!!!

If you are the type of person who is curious and determined, who will buy a magic trick and practice and practice it, to get it right, then I would love to hear your story, and I am sure I would love to help - so please read on! If you are not that type of person, in my eyes you are a CANT. And therefore, please email me if you can't return this book, and I will refund what you've paid.

BUT, if you have even the slightest curiosity as to whether you might be able to change, carry on reading.

If you do not change your attitude after you've finished, I will still refund your money.

Good deal?

The Disco Story

In my early teenage years, the disco was the place to be. Always in a big hall, the D.J. at one end, boys on one side, girls on the other and all those hormones buzzing in-between.

It was 'the Agony and the Ecstasy' at the same time. To begin with there was more agony than ecstasy and that was because in my mind, asking a girl for a dance was

'Committing to the Impossible' and I hadn't worked it out - I hadn't worked out the Belief, Strategy and Capability.

It is always a good idea to imitate someone who has done the impossible and so I asked the advice of an older lad. He was nothing special to look at but he was streetwise, he was cool - and he always got his dance! I used to ask him, "How do you do it?"

"I'm a 'Main Boy!' " he replied. I remember acting like him, dressing like him, I remember asking him, "Am I a 'Main Boy?' "

He always said, "Frank, you are not 'A Main Boy!' "

Then one day, when I asked him (again), "Adam, am I a 'Main Boy?' "

He replied "Frank, the day you stop asking is the day you are a 'Main Boy!' "

I didn't get it at first and then it dawned on me. The day I stop asking is the day when I truly have 'Belief'! So I stopped asking. Step 1: Belief - sorted.

The 2nd step was to work out my Strategy. Now, everyone knows you never ask the prettiest girl, because she's bound to be out of your league; she might say no (and so say all the CANTS). So no one asks them, and they stand there all night wondering "Why doesn't anyone ask me for a dance?" So, my strategy was to ask the prettiest girl for a dance (CAN!).

The 3rd step: Capability - This comes down to practice, practice, practice! In other words, continue to ask the prettiest girls for a dance and develop my capability in doing so. And the more you practice these techniques, the less you behave like a CANT.

And it worked! Now, I do not mean that all of the prettiest girls were falling over me asking me for dates, but I did dance with them and we used to have really good fun because they just wanted to have a chat and a good time - nothing more, nothing less.

I look back at my disco days and see how much I learnt in terms of 'Commit to the Impossible' and the value of your belief, working out your strategy and building your capability through practice. And of course, once you commit, it does not seem so 'Impossible'!

Rule 1
YOU CAN GET THE ESSENCE

Get the Best out of life

Nobody cares how you do things anymore. Everyone expects what they expect, and they expect it <u>now</u>. I think Amazon is probably to be blamed/ credited/ applauded for this.

What people actually want to know is WHY you do it.

The WHY is your Essence.

I like the idea of the 'LYNX™ EFFECT', and not because it's the fragrance that allegedly makes you attractive to men or women, but because it brings out your essence - and that's why people are drawn to you. Everyone has a diamond inside that needs to be admired, it's just over time we have all too often covered it in crap and it has become less visible. Clean it up, and your essence will shine. Some people (e.g. Nikki Owen - famed for the 'Big Apple Experiment') call this your **Charisma**.

There are three ways 'YOU CAN GET THE ESSENCE'. These are outlined in Chapters 1 - 3.

Chapter 1 What is the point? Get CONTEXT in your life.

Chapter 2 Why do this? Have a PURPOSE to your life.

Chapter 3 Less is more. Be more EFFECTIVE in your life.

Chapter 1
What's the Point? Get CONTEXT[1] in your life.

"If you look after the pounds the pennies will look after themselves." Me

I don't know about you, but I quickly get extremely bored, especially if someone doesn't get to the point in a short period of time. I've even been known to say, "I'm bored now; I have to go!" Even though that's quite funny (well, at least for me), I do really feel that way sometimes.

In an age when time is of the essence, getting very quickly to the point and staying there is really important to me. 'The point' brings a common topic into conversations for everyone to stay aligned with and orient to, so we can all stay on track.

If you concentrate on the CONTEXT, the CONTENT will look after itself.

Clarity, Focus and Time

Have you ever found yourself in a situation where you felt you weren't really getting to the point? Perhaps you were in a meeting, and it seemed to meander? It went on longer than you expected, and no one was really clear about the outcomes?

When that happens, there is a knock-on effect because afterwards, you find yourself spending even more of your time trying to get clear on what's expected from you and what others are supposed to be doing. Or even worse nothing happens until the next meeting, when folk just look at each other and say, "What was it we discussed last time? What did we agree?" That way nothing gets done - because you're in a room full of CANTS!

How would you like to get clarity in all aspects of your life? To be focussed not in a driven way but in a calm, effortless way, making the best use of your time? Well you can, simply by consistently applying 'What's the point?' - not in an argumentative, downhearted way but in an inquisitive, excited manner. This will give you clarity and focus, save you time and enable your day-to-day activities to have purpose.

If you keep on asking and you still don't get the CONTEXT, you're in the presence of a bunch of CANTS, and you have my permission to say, "I'm bored now" and walk away. If you have the patience to carry on for a little longer, you can try seeing it from their point of view. This may give you not only another CONTEXT but also clarity around your own CONTEXT, but a lot of the time this just muddies the waters - and, if you get too bogged down in CONTENT, you may have to do some serious CHUNKING UP to get back to your CONTEXT. ☺

Chunking Up[2]

At some stage, everyone finds themselves bogged down with detail and unable to see the wood for the trees. The process of CHUNKING UP allows you to get out of that unproductive, frustrating state quickly. It removes those blinkers, so you can see the big picture.

Let me give you an example. Suppose you make a salami sandwich (and if you're vegetarian, imagine making one for your worst enemy). You open the fridge and take out a slice of salami.

Chunking up a level, you see that the salami is part of a packet of salami slices.

Chunking up again, the slices come from a big long sausage thing.

Up again, the sausage thing comes from a haunch of meat.

Which comes from a pig. Get it? Chunking up takes you from the detail to the big picture. It's the opposite of the old adage about eating an elephant one bite at a time (which is also not a good example for vegetarians)!

When we chunk up in our lives, we ask ourselves questions to take us away from detail and to the big picture:

- What would this result in?
- What's this a part of?
- What's the intention here?
- What purpose does this serve?
- What will this achieve?
- Where will this take me?

CHUNKING UP

The more you chunk up, the more you can get a grasp on the CONTEXT. Once you have the context (if you need to), you can always chunk back down to get the detail - but when you chunk back down, don't be surprised if you find your details aren't exactly what you thought they were! You'll be seeing them in the light of the bigger context. That salami might not look nearly so appealing if you have a fondness for pigs…

So, in this example, thinking about where your salami originated (the pig), you might then decide that - when you chunk all the way back down to choosing your sandwich filling - you go for the vegetarian option!

Or you'll remain totally ok with where salami comes from, and make the same (but better informed) decision. And, in its simplest form, that's what chunking up can do - give you the context to make better decisions, or to check your decisions. Of course, if you have sorted your context in the first place, you'd automatically know what sandwich you were having anyway ;)

If you chunk things up enough, you will be able to reach a simple understanding of context - a place where everybody understands the point or purpose of something.

For instance, you may have two people building a wall. One thinks, "I am building a wall," and doesn't focus on anything else. The other knows that, while he is also building the wall, that is just a part of the house they are building. He has the context/focus of building a house or even a higher context of building a home.

At my business, Bastows, everyone has their individual role to play - but everyone knows that their work all goes towards 'making London beautiful'. More on that in a bit.

In summary: if you have a different context from someone else you hang around with, you have a different focus - for example, if you're a natural giver and you hang around with takers, this is gonna be a problem.

If you are a CAN and you hang around with CANTS, what does that make you?

Source and Outcome[3]

Understanding both the SOURCE and the OUTCOME are critical to successful communication and understanding context.

The SOURCE is what is really behind the issue… it's the source of the problem, or the energy behind it. The OUTCOME is the result of the problem.

My son fell off his bike (again) last week. The OUTCOME was a crack on the head and a skinned knee. The SOURCE was a tyre with a slow leak. So giving him an aspirin and dressing the scrape is just fixing the outcome, and won't resolve the problem. Fixing the outcome(s) is what I like to call the 'sticking plaster solution' (for obvious reasons), and when you simply try to do this, all too often nothing actually gets resolved. If all you do is buy sticking plasters, you're being a silly CANT. You need to fix the puncture (identify the SOURCE) or the OUTCOME will stay the same.

How about this? Are you familiar with this conversation? "What's wrong now? I brought you flowers. You said I never buy you flowers," (for flowers, feel free to substitute whatever). You fixed the outcome, not the source of the complaint (and just for the record, saying "I love you" lasts longer than a bunch of roses, and it's a lot cheaper, too).

Sometimes there can be more than one source - or can

there? Let's say you have an issue with high staff turnover. This isn't a problem, it's an OUTCOME, and there are several potential sources for it: Poor recruiting. Low morale. Bad management. Lack of good training.

You could deal with/fix each of these sources to change the outcome. Or, you could just chunk up to find the REAL source. There might be an issue with where the buck stops: is the big cheese (that's you) setting the example and standard needed to create a happy company that staff love working for? I've had to take some long hard looks at myself in the past, and make some changes where necessary. The key was finding my own context.

My Context

I've got a huge respect for my Father, who was a giant of a man and ex-rugby player - but he was also a very difficult man at times. I first discovered the context in my life when I was working 14 hours a day (including Saturdays) in my Dad's slave force.

On one occasion, I came in to the office after a particularly long, tough day and my Dad was on the computer. Let's just say we had words; I can't even remember what about. He said, "Don't you ever talk to me like that!" For the first time in my life I got hold of him, swung him around, yanked him onto his feet, and said, "Don't you ever talk to me like that again! I'm busting my back for this company.

Don't ever say that again!" I dropped him and ran out in tears.

I was driving back home when I looked at myself in the mirror, and my eyes were all watery. I pulled over to the side of the road because I couldn't drive and I couldn't breathe, and my entire insides felt full of acid. I suddenly thought, "I'm having a heart attack!" People were stopping and saying, "Are you alright?" and I said, "I think I'm having a heart attack…"

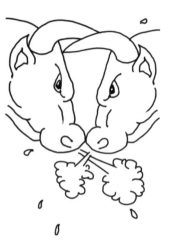

After a while I calmed down and went home, where my Wife said, "Right; you look like death! We're taking you to the hospital." I only found out later, when watching someone go through the same thing on an episode of 'The Sopranos' that I'd had a panic attack, but it felt like a real heart attack. That was when I said to myself, "No; that's enough."

When we'd both calmed down, I asked the old man, "When am I going to take over this business? Because right now

I'm putting all I have into it, without so much as a thank you." He looked me straight in the eye and said, "As long as I'm alive, you'll never run this f***ing business!" So I knew that was it, and I wasn't sticking around. Just like that, I went. I was finally being a CAN.

From there on, it was really hard. I think my Dad wanted me to fail so I could come back under his wing, but I didn't. I borrowed £10k from somebody I knew and set myself up in Fulham, in a little basement with one desk. My own building refurbishment business. It was then that I realised I wasn't working for my Dad any more, and I just started smiling. I realised that I was actually creating a Universe for myself, and that was the first time I got context in my life.

My context was happiness. It was happiness that I was looking for, but the source was creating my own Universe. Creating my own Universe gave me happiness. The SOURCE was creating my own universe, the OUTCOME was happiness. There was nobody else to blame now. If things went right, it was down to me. If things went wrong, it was down to me. And that was exactly how I wanted it.

It would have been easy for me to stay under my Dad's wing. No risk. Staying in my comfort zone.

I realise now that you need to do the right thing, and not the easy thing. If you like, I had to deal with the SOURCE of my unhappiness, and not just the OUTCOME of that situation (which would have meant stagnating, *swallowing my unhappiness and putting up with my 'rough deal').*

*Looking back, I can see that my solution, difficult and long term as it was, did two things. It fulfilled my intent and answered my **WHY**. (More on **WHY** in a moment). And it sorted me out for the long term! It wasn't the easy thing to do, but it was the right thing to do.*

Summary

Context is everything in communication. Without context, the same thing often has two (or more) entirely different meanings. Clear understanding of the context creates deeper and more meaningful relationships.

People who insist on communicating without context can be right CANTS, they confuse everything and waste time. They just make noise and steal your energy.

Relationships lead to the life of your dreams. Stronger business relationships translate to more sales and higher profit margins, which brings more money to take care of your family. Stronger personal relationships mean less stress and arguments.

But finding the context or the point of your life is only the first step. Next, we take a closer look at finding the purpose or the **WHY** behind why you do what you do.

Next steps

1. ☐

2. ☐

3. ☐

Refs: [1][2][3] Context and Source Outcome are Frameworks and Chunking Up is a concept used by kind permission of Shirlaws - Please also refer to page 80.

" I AM THE GREATEST "

"I said that even before I knew I was."

Muhammad Ali

Clarity, Focus and Time

Everything you do has a reason behind it, whether you're aware of it or not - and I do mean **everything**.

Your reason for it all is your **WHY**. It might be as simple as, "I'm going to bed early so I feel good for my big meeting tomorrow." Or it could be as complex as, "I'm doing this because it allows me to leave my children financially secure." Or as personal as, "Because it feels good." There's always a **WHY** somewhere.

Your **WHY** needs to be the big picture reason for why you're doing what you're doing in life. Get the **WHY** right, and you'll always stay on track.

WHY I Get Up in the Morning

I was looking for my **WHY**, my INTENT[1], my "this makes me want to jump out of bed in the morning." But I hated what answer I came up with, even though my interpretation of the word was different to that of others.

My intent or purpose (my **WHY**) was 'TO PERFECT'. You can see my problem….

I lived with it for 6 months until a friend suggested a better word. I've lived with his suggestion for the last 5 years, and it still makes me happy.

'To Beautify'

Perfection was an unattainable and subjective dream, but I could get great satisfaction making a situation more beautiful.

As long as I help to leave a situation, person, place or whatever a little bit more beautiful than it was before, I'm happy. 'To beautify' may sound woolly, and if any of you have ever met me, 'woolly' wouldn't be a word you'd use to describe me, but to beautify is the essence of what makes me happy.

By the way, our **WHY** should never be 'perfection' - to be perfect. Like Ali, we can be the best, but we will never obtain perfection. Humanity is by definition a work in progress (just ask Cher's plastic surgeon).

As humans we always want more. So even if we have a clearly defined picture of what perfection means to us, and we obtain it, someone else will go ahead and say it's not perfect and off we go again. It's a cycle many young women are trapped in; trying to be thinner and thinner, or prettier and prettier, and you know where those sad stories end up.

Trying to be perfect only sets you up for failure every time, because perfection isn't doing something without mistakes, it's doing the best you can with what you have and learning to find whatever your own 'perfect' is. Perfection is subjective, and you'll never live up to your own standards of perfection, let alone someone else's.

Striving for beautification is a far more wonderful way to look at life. By striving to beautify everything we come in contact with in some way, we can rest easy, knowing we've accomplished something without driving ourselves crazy trying to attain something that not only seems impossible, but actually is.

Summary

Without a clearly defined **WHY** to motivate us, it's easy to get derailed. Always ask yourself: "**WHY** are you doing what you're doing?" When you know your **WHY**, it's far easier to go out and 'just do it!'

So when you know your **WHY**, it's time to take a closer look at how to be more effective in life. We all have a finite amount of time here on this Earth and we never know when our time is up, so make the most of the time you have by increasing your effectiveness. Question: is it worth your while learning to identify your **WHY**? (Clue: Don't be a CANT!).

Next steps

1.   ☐

2.   ☐

3.   ☐

Ref:[1] Intent is a Framework used by kind permission of Shirlaws - Please also refer to page 80.

Chapter 3
Less is more.   Be more effective in your life.

The 80/20 Rule

Nobody can add more hours to the day. When we get up in the morning, we have exactly the same number of hours, minutes and seconds at our disposal as Richard Branson. The difference between us all is what we do with them.

The **80/20 Rule** (also known as the Pareto Principle) is critical to increasing your effectiveness. **80%** of your effort will net you **20%** of your results. So go find that

20% of effort that will give you **80%** of your results! Focus your time and effort on the things that really matter and will achieve the most. Don't get caught up in the rest.

If **20%** of your staff produces **80%** of the results then pay them more - they're worth every penny. If **20%** of your mistakes cause **80%** of the hassle in your life, fix what needs to be fixed. If **20%** of your customers contribute **80%** of your revenue, make sure those customers are kept happy and feel good about buying from you. Then develop more of them.

So what do you do with the clients that are causing you grief? Fire them (yes, really)! You don't have to work with everybody that wants you. Pick and choose, and only work with the people you want to work with - the ones that give you the best reward.

Get it right, and you can spend a lot less time behind your desk if you're getting far more done when you are there.

Apply this principle to all areas of your life, and you'll see dramatic improvement in your quality of life. It's simple! Do you want to spend your valuable time with CANS or CANTS?

Are You the Weakest Link?

There's a saying I'll bet you've heard many times; "a team is only as strong as it's weakest link." Well, that's a load of old crap!

A team can be as strong as it's strongest link. That one strong link can inspire, motivate, kick into touch and train the weaker links, until they come up to the same standard. That one strong link is your **20%**.

Our Local Senior School

Everyone concentrates on the weakest link. The Headmaster of our local Senior School concentrates on the strongest link to bring everyone else up.

He only does 3 things (**20%** of what could be done) to get **80%** effect.

1. He goes in to every class every day unannounced, and asks a question of the teacher and a random pupil by name - this keeps everyone doing their best for the whole day.

2. Each subject has three streamed classes, and he gets the best teachers to teach the smaller, less talented classes and the less able teachers to teach the best classes. This way, the bottom level is quickly raised to a higher level.

3. He really believes that if you believe you are a winner and dress like one, you will be a winner. So he has a non-negotiable. Everyone must look immaculate in school uniform every day, and the teachers are told to dress like they're going to a wedding. Every day.

He's been there for 18 months, in which time he's sacked and changed 28 teachers (luckily he has the backing of the governors!). He has taken the school from a failing school to one of the highest achieving schools in Surrey for GCSE's and A levels, and which had over 5000 prospective parents and pupils viewing at a recent 'open weekend' (as at 2013).

Summary

With so many things demanding our attention every day, productivity and effectiveness are key to success. The **80/20 rule** means you only select the right things to do; the ones that get the biggest results possible. Then that **80%** of your time is free to do the things you LIKE doing.

Focusing on the strongest link allows you to use the 'trickle-down effect' to bump up those weaker links. Never focus on the negative in an attempt to make it as strong as the positive (haven't you heard of flogging a dead horse?).

At this point, you now have everything you need to

master the first rule - YOU CAN GET THE ESSENCE.
(Personal & business CONTEXT, and identifying your
WHY).

Now it's time to move on to the second rule - YOU CAN
GET THE ENERGY.

Next steps

1. ☐

2. ☐

3. ☐

Rule 2
YOU CAN GET THE ENERGY

Get the energy you need out of life

Imagine you are a computer. You're powered by electrical energy, and as long as that energy is clean and doesn't peak or fall, you run beautifully.

Getting yourself to run beautifully is what this section is all about.

There are three ways 'YOU CAN GET THE ENERGY', as outlined here in Chapters 4 to 6.

Chapter 4 Stay off the triangle.

Chapter 5 Get Balance and Alignment in your world.

Chapter 6 Differentiate spilt milk and crossed bridges.

Chapter 4
Stay off the triangle

"It takes a great deal of courage to stand up to your enemies, but a great deal more to stand up to your friends." **Dumbledore (aka J K Rowling)**

"Try not to do anything stupid." **Daniel Negranu's Mum – World class poker player (that's Daniel, not his Mum)**

"The problem is not the problem.
The problem is your attitude about the problem.
Do you understand?"

Capt Jack Sparrow

Stay off the Triangle

Take a look at the diagram below.

Are you a **HERO**? "I can do that!"

A **VILLAIN**? "Let's see how they like it…"

A **VICTIM**? "Why does it always happen to me?"

Well, to avoid falling into any of these, stay off the triangle.

So how **do** you stay off the triangle?

Well, I operate as much as possible from what I call the Circle of Clarity - in the centre. This is where I make my best decisions, have my clarity of thought and have "clean energy". Sure, I **pretend** to be the hero, the victim or the villain at times (when it's useful), but in that circle of clarity is where I see clear solutions without all the baggage.

One of the things I will often do is act out a particular situation in my mind's eye from each role, playing the hero, the villain and then the victim. Then I get into the circle of clarity with all that insight, and THEN I choose what to do. It's a great way to make decisions.

My poker triangle

I love Tournament Poker, because it's just like creating a new business. You start off with a small stack of chips, and you build up as you go on as the blinds get bigger. You either double your stack, increase it and then win, or you lose all your money and go bust.

But Poker isn't just a game of skill and learning about the odds. It's a people game, and so

long as you can work out what other people have in their hand, what you've got in your own hand doesn't much matter. So I use the drama triangle all the time. There are 3 types of poker player you can take advantage of in a bad situation.

There are those that have just had a ridiculously bad bit of luck and been knocked out or lost half of their chips. They're victims. "Why does it always happen to me? Why am I always the one? Why do I always have so much bad luck?"

Other people accumulate a lot of chips and end up bullying everybody. Now bullying is good play in a way, but you should be constructive with it. When these people get a massive amount of chips they can accumulate massive villainy wealth. Villains, "Yah suckers!"

Then there are the heroes - and they're very rare in poker, because of the old saying, 'Don't give a sucker an even break'. These people don't take advantage of the ignorance or naïvety of newcomers, and they give them a break. Sound good? Well, I can't count the amount of times I've seen this happen. "Well I won't call you on that, even though I could knock you out and bust you". They do this because they want to cut them some slack as they're new/unlucky/naïve/hard up/pretty. A lot of the time, these new players end up winning because they've been given some leeway, and they don't care/know they've been given a break. They just think they're clever.

I've won and cashed in some of the biggest poker events in the world, and I've realised that none of those 3 places is the one to be in. I stay off the triangle. In the circle of clarity I can see all these people. I'm 'in the zone' if you like, or 'in flow' or whatever you like to call it. It doesn't mean I can't turn into a victim, villain or hero, but I don't. In fact, it's a good sneaky technique; acting out a role without being in that role.

I might get called on a big stack, and be called a villain. But I don't take it personally. I sometimes pretend to be the hero and put down a massive hand because I like the person, and so maybe later he'll let me get away with something. But I'm not being kind, I just don't have the hand and I knew he was going to call me.

Sometimes I love playing the victim, because if I've just been outdrawn and been unlucky in the hand, often I shortly end up with a massive hand. When you just push in all your chips after a massive hand everybody thinks, "Ahhhh! He's down", and they'll call you with the weakest of hands. Then when you turn over aces, they're done for and you get to check up.

There's a saying in poker: "The best way of getting off tilt is by putting somebody else on tilt."

Poker can be just a bit of fun, but staying off the drama triangle means you CAN handle all the luck, good and bad, that the game throws at you - and, funnily enough, that works for everything in that other big game - the game of life. Rudyard Kipling knew what I'm on about. He definitely wasn't a CANT.

Summary

Don't ever get caught up in the triangle - unless it's in the centre. Being a villain doesn't inspire trust and good will. Being a victim doesn't gain respect and trust. Being a hero may seem nice but it creates a rod for your own back and allows others to slip into victim mode all too easily.

Next steps

1.   ☐

2.   ☐

3.   ☐

Chapter 5
Get Balance and Alignment in your world

"The biggest decision you will ever make in your life is the people you decide to hang around with."
Some fat bald bloke who wrote this book

"Real integrity is doing the right thing, knowing that nobody's going to know whether you did it or not."
Oprah Winfrey

We'll talk about personal energy later on, but for now, here's a little tool I've found can help.

Accept it, change it or remove it.

The easy mnemonic is AICIRI ☺

REPEAT AFTER ME

There are only three things you can do in a conflict situation:

ACCEPT IT   CHANGE IT   REMOVE IT

And by the way, 'remove it' doesn't necessarily mean getting a hit man to solve your problems! Rather than getting rid of someone, sometimes you can remove his or her problem to resolve the situation.

Not choosing one of the above 3 options only leads to misery. Choosing any one of them (take your pick) is far better for your energy in the long run.

Balance and Alignment

BALANCE is when you're in that circle of clarity we just talked about. We all talk about 'the work life balance'; so much so that it's become a cliché. Yet more balance is what we all need (unless you're the Dalai Lama).

ALIGNMENT is the thing that pulls on your balance. It exerts positive or negative force, helping or hindering your efforts at balance. The worst thing you can do is to align yourself with the wrong people, whether in your personal or professional life.

If you surround yourself with people who don't make you happy, who don't challenge you to be the best version of yourself or who use you, then you'll only become tired, unmotivated and bitter. Your energy will be sucked away, you'll be off-balance and eventually you'll move backwards or spin your wheels doing nothing. Making you (yes, you've guessed it) a CANT.

Remember the **80/20 rule** in your relationships; they're about quality, not quantity. Henry the VIII had 6 wives. Now that's my version of getting the **80/20 rule** arse about face!

Conversely, if you're aligned with the right people, you're surrounding yourself with those you can learn from. They'll support you in your endeavours and push you to do more - and do it better. You'll feel a positive change in your energy. You'll be motivated to progress and happy to participate. You'll be aligned and balanced… which increases your energy.

So hang on to that **20%** of people in your life that give you **80%** of the reward.

Think Feel Know[1]

We process information through THINKING, FEELING and KNOWING. These are the ways we communicate with others, and working out which one you have a tendency to use over others can be extremely helpful.

Moreover, identifying another person's process can help you align with them, setting up a good relationship with minimal effort.

Do you like to analyse pros and cons, logically make your decisions and try to remain impersonal, putting personal feelings aside?

Then you're Mr Spock. A THINKER.

Or are you always willing to do whatever it takes to establish harmony, concerned with what's best for all the people involved, always being caring and tactful. That's right, you're a FEELER.

Me, I'm a KNOWER. I go with my gut feeling. I know what needs to be done, and I don't need to think or feel to know the decision I've made is right. By the way, most knowers actually go through thinking and feeling first. But they do it in the blink of an eye, and THEN they know. But beware of 'bad knowers', because there are good knowers (like me!) and bad knowers - the ones who are dogmatic, or who make snap decisions without the facts. Try to avoid those. They can be really awful CANTS. Because they THINK they CAN!

Of course, everyone actually uses a combination of the three, and some decisions are best handled by changing style. Using the THINK, FEEL, KNOW principles can help you to understand your customers and friends. If they're thinkers, talk to them with your thinking self. You'll sell more effectively. If they're feelers, talk feeling to them. You'll build relationships with customers more effectively. If they're knowers, try to convince and persuade them with logic. You'll reduce and eliminate conflict.

Get it?

Brave, Harmonious and True
Making London Beautiful[2]

My main business (and the one I love most) is called 'Bastows'. I told you earlier how I identified my intent or purpose - my **WHY** - it's 'To Beautify'. This came from work I did on 'values' in the business. From those same values came the concept of the business 'To Nurture'. It fits perfectly with a family feel we have in the company.

It's really important to remember that the words themselves are not our Values - what's important is what those words mean to us. As long as the values' words have been thoroughly discussed, they'll be a cue for triggering a way of behaving and living.

For Bastows, those words are Brave, Harmonious and True.

When we are BRAVE, we are supportive, assuring, innovative, confident, challenging, coaching, leading.

When we are HARMONIOUS, we know what we're doing. We are professional, aligned, together and we work at source. However, Harmonious doesn't mean always working together in a quiet and calm fashion. It can also mean being energetic or angry - but the fact that we're all energetic and angry together means we're 'in harmony'; we're all on the same page.

That's true harmony.

When we are TRUE, we are honest, trusted and trusting, open, fair, forgiving, caring, happy and passionate.

These are just some of the behaviours we identify with being Brave, Harmonious and True, and we live by them every day. These aren't words on a plaque at Head Office; we carry them in our hearts, minds and bodies. We live and breathe them within the Bastows Family, and with our suppliers, clients and tenants.

That's what being 'Value-driven' is really about.

Coincidentally, Bastows Vision is 'To Make London Beautiful.' Which is remarkably close to my own personal purpose 'To Beautify'. Funny, that . . . .

Summary

Before you can be truly happy and productive you need to be able to find, create, or restore balance by removing conflict from your life. This creates a positive energy, pulling you toward success.

This sometimes means you have to cut relationships with things and people toxic to you. Or, to put it another way, CANTS. Align yourself with the right people, and remove yourself from the wrong people or situation. Do a relationship assessment. What value do they bring to your life? What do you get from them? Are you giving more than you get? Is the balance in line? If not, move on!

Make yourself value-driven, and the success will follow.

Next, we'll talk about not living a life of regret, and how to seize every moment and make the most of it.

Next steps

1. ☐

2. ☐

3. ☐

Ref:[1] THINK FEEL KNOW is a Framework used by kind permission of Shirlaws

Ref:[2] 'Making London Beautiful' arose from a 'Positioning' exercise with Shirlaws - Please also refer to page 80.

Chapter 6
Let's talk about spilt milk and crossed bridges

'I'm ashamed, but I don't regret it !!!'
Nick Moorbath – Music legend and a genuine loveable rogue.

"What is past is past. Never go back. Not for excuses. Not for justification, not for happiness. You are what you are, the world is what it is." Mario Puzo, 'The Last Don'

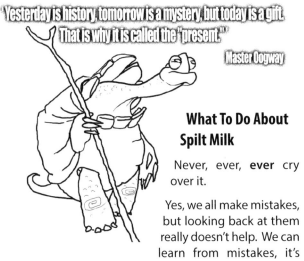

"Yesterday is history, tomorrow is a mystery, but today is a gift. That is why it is called the "present.""

Master Oogway

What To Do About Spilt Milk

Never, ever, **ever** cry over it.

Yes, we all make mistakes, but looking back at them really doesn't help. We can learn from mistakes, it's true, but generally speaking what is done is done. Allow yourself a short period of time to analyse what happened, how it happened, and whether you can learn anything from it. Then move on. Do not dwell! It's unproductive, even destructive. Just get over it.

Crossing Bridges

When you cross a bridge, you leave the other side behind. In life, don't cross bridges lightly and when you do, be prepared for the possibility that they've burned behind you. Don't faff about going back and forth, back and forth, waiting for that magical conviction you're going the right way.

Cross, and have done with it. Keep separate things separate. That was then, this is now, so get on with it and make it work.

Day Tight Compartments

Do you know people who worry about every little thing? The solution is living in 'day tight compartments'. These help you focus on **the present**.

Most people look forward to the future, and are driven/guided by the past. They make decisions based on a heady cocktail of past experience and future projection. They worry about spilt milk, and try to avoid crossing bridges.

It's no wonder that few people are actually PRESENT in **the present**.

A day tight compartment means not looking to the past, or more than 24 hours into the future. You live in the present and focus on the task at hand. Live each day until bedtime, without thinking back or forward. This allows you to use your energy and motivation in the here and now, free of external influences.

It's '**presentology**', and I practice it whenever I can.

And for those times when you find yourself completely overwhelmed (and we all have them), just ask yourself "What's the worst that could happen?" Accept it, and everything else is a bonus!

Live every day as if it were your last. Savour the moment. Tomorrow gets its turn tomorrow, and yesterday had its chance already!

Lose track of time (yes, I really did say that). Immerse yourself in everything you do to the point where you're unaware of anything else. Trust me, if it's important enough, it'll make itself noticed.

Never stop living in the now. Live, don't think. Avoid "autopilot." Start paying attention to new things. Take new routes to work. Make different things for dinner. Embrace new. Get busy! Focus on what you do and it'll naturally push everything else into the background.

Facing a Financial Meltdown Story

In January 1999 I was sitting at my desk and for a moment (just for a moment) a numbing sensation shot through my body - I was down £1.2 million!

Our business had been doing well and, ever the investor, I'd been building up a property portfolio. The plan was to generate income over a period of time and then realise the capital assets through sale.

The property market had been a bit turbulent, so I thought I'd check the portfolio's asset value against the liabilities; essentially the bank loans and mortgages.

As I completed the figures, I realised that the bank loans and mortgages were more than the value of the properties, and if all of the creditors suddenly said, "repay your loans" I'd lose £1.2 million. Essentially, everything I'd worked for - and more.

What to do? I could have continued to sit and stare at the figures and worried myself silly. Or phoned the banks and mortgage companies, told them of my plight, worn sackcloth and ashes and accepted crushing financial defeat. But that's not my style. That's what a CANT would do - crying over the spilt milk! So I decided to live in the present moment, because that's all I have influence over - and when you look at it like that, it's a big ALL!

I put together a game plan. I looked at what properties I could sell to minimise my exposure, and I did it step by step without resorting to a fire sale. First of all, I looked at a bungalow which had 2 plots beside it. I thought maybe I could raise £120,000, which was what I owed on it. It went to auction and raised £270,000.

Then there was another house I'd bought with a view to getting planning permission on the plot to build a bigger house. The planning permission came through, and the value of the plot went from £380,000 to £750,000! And so it went on. I felt as if I had the Midas touch!

*What had happened was that I'd checked the asset value of my property portfolio at a deep low, and now the market was coming back. By living in the present moment and in day tight compartments, I'd held my nerve and been able to make the right decisions - **and** suffer no stress during the process. I accepted the worst possible situation (remember AICIRI ☺), and worked on improving it.*

You can't live in fear if you're grateful!

Summary

We tend to let our thoughts consume us. We dwell on the past and what we could have done differently to change where we are today. We're stuffed full of "what ifs…" and "wish I's…". We focus on the future, because we want to make sure what we're doing right now will be enough to get us to where we want to go. It's natural, but that doesn't mean it's the right thing to do.

I for one don't want to wake up one day and wonder where my life went, finding it was sucked right out of me, even though I'm still breathing! But when we let thoughts of our past or future consume us, we lose today - and when we lose today, we've lost life.

That's why using day tight compartments embraces the present and focuses on it. There's no sense in dwelling on the past. We are where we are.

Live every day as if it were your last. The present is what really matters.

Next steps

1. ☐

2. ☐

3. ☐

Rule 3
YOU CAN GET THE IMPOSSIBLE

Get what you want from this life

You can do anything you set your mind to. As clichéd as it may sound, it's the truth. YOU are your BIGGEST obstacle. Establish your non-negotiables, and make sure you don't allow them into your life.

Now that you've gotten your essence, and you've discovered how to make your life run beautifully, it's time to reach out and grab life by the horns.

To get what you want - no matter how impossible it may seem.

There are three ways 'YOU CAN GET THE IMPOSSIBLE', as outlined in Chapters 7 to 9.

Chapter 7 Do terrifying and exciting stuff.

Chapter 8 It's great to be in the zone.

Chapter 9 Steal from the best and leave the rest.

Chapter 7
Do terrifying and exciting stuff

"Life Begins at the End of Your Comfort Zone"
Neale Donald Walsch

"You're best to apologise afterwards rather than ask permission beforehand." Anon

"Break the Rules." Richard Branson

"And now, Harry, let us step out into the night and pursue that flighty temptress, adventure." Dumbledore (aka J K Rowling)

Just Start and Say Yes!

Never allow yourself to become bored with life and your goals. Yes, most people would like a good job, family, nice home, fast car, etc. But think BIG. Really big. Strive for more!

Make a bucket list - a list of things to do before you die (kick the bucket!). If you have one already, check it. How many of those things have you done? What's stopping you? Are you afraid to go outside your comfort zone? If you answered yes to that last question, you're not truly living. You are, in fact, being a bit of a CANT.

Make your bucket list contain at least 3 big things that are exciting and terrifying (to you) that will take you out of your comfort zone and make you learn new things and improve your body and mind. David Hyner (famous for the 'Rhino Concept') argues that they should be awesome and ridiculous. And make them flexible, contextual goals, too, replacing them when completed or when they don't excite you anymore.

I had 3 goals on my bucket list while writing this book. The first was to run or walk 100 miles in 24 hours. This put focus on my health and would satisfy my desire to raise money for a great cause. The second was to produce a film. This would satisfy my love of film, and make me do something I've never done before and wished I could. Finally, to win a major poker tournament. Poker still seems to be the only hobby I have not lost interest in over many years and I still believe that I have it in me to win and become world champion. The mastery and endurance of this act would help and strengthen other areas of my life.

The worst thing you can do is to allow yourself to stagnate. Yes, celebrate your accomplishment when you reach a goal, but for heaven's sake **don't stop!** Find something new to strive for - something even bigger. When you stop having goals, you stop living.

Don't let the pressure of having a goal and figuring out how to achieve it slow you down or stop you. At all costs, don't get stuck in 'analysis paralysis', where you're constantly planning but never taking action. Remember, chunk up. Learn to enjoy that pressure. It's good for you. It's helping you learn and grow as a person.

Take action. Learn to say YES. Get your ass off the couch and just START, because nothing will change if you don't.

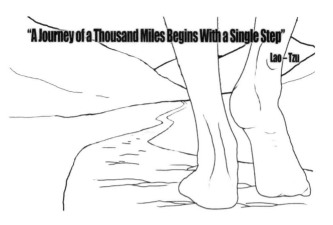

"A Journey of a Thousand Miles Begins With a Single Step"

Lao – Tzu

My journey of a thousand miles… (well, 100 km)

*I hit 50. I shouldn't be smoking, I was eating too much, I **used** to be super fit. So I publicly committed to dropping weight. Well, I got down to 15 stone, and then I told everyone I was now going to stop smoking. But 9 months later, sadly (if predictably), the weight had all gone back on.*

So I committed to something POSITIVE - to get fitter - and decided to do it not just for myself, but to help others. I took on the 100km challenge, for the Construction Youth Trust, and ended up raising £7k for them. However, thinking big, I went and told everyone I wanted to do it within 24 hours. A lot of people said they would double their pledge if I really did do it in 24 hours, which is of course always a good sign that they think you're going mad.

I trained up to 26 kilometres a day, was fit and rubbed my feet with surgical spirit so they got harder. 100 km seemed like it would be just fine.

Well… The first 50 km I did in less than 10 hours, and I didn't even go that fast because a mate did the first 25 with me, and in fact I slowed down to help him out. Then I left him and went on to do the 50 km, having a massage at the 50th. Actually, it was pretty easy. "24 hours? Piece of cake!" I thought to myself. So I said, "Do you know what? I'm going to do the 100 in under 20 hours."

By the next stop I had some blisters, so I poked those and bandaged them up. It got to 18 km from the end and I was tearing along, when all of a sudden it felt like someone had stuck a knife in my big toe. I had a bad blister already and I was OK with that, but now I had a blister on a blister. But from here I could actually see the next stage, so I thought, "What the hell? I'm only 4k away…"

Well, it took me 2 hours to stumble just 4 km to the next station, where they looked at my foot and said, "Man, you're going to hospital to get this stitched." But I said, "No way! I need to finish this one in 24 hours." So they bandaged it all up. I'd run out of supports and they didn't have any more, so now I was in real pain and I told them, "This one you'd better pop and bandage it up." But they didn't want to touch that one!

Because of the 4 km when I'd been walking wrongly, both my heels had now developed blisters. So they bandaged everything up and stuck my feet back in my boots, and although I was already in pain, I could feel this one blister that was really bad.

So I left there and ploughed on, getting to 90 km. Just 10 km to go, when I went over a bridge, stumbled and the

blister went. It hurt so much I just chucked up over the side of the bridge. I went into my bull-headed mindset and said to myself, "I'm not looking in my boot! I've got 10 km to go, I've got to finish this within 24 hours. Just keep on going, Frank."

That was bad enough, but every now and then I clunked my foot, and all of a sudden the agony came back, so I just tried to go to a happy place. The sun came out (which always helps), and in the sunshine I went through a field where there were about a hundred cows - and one great big bull! He was looking right at me and I thought, "I can't run; I can't go any further. Happy place, happy place! I'm in my happy place!"

Of course I got past it and kind of regenerated, when the hills started. Unbelievable: why did they have the hills at the end, rather than at the beginning? But eventually I did it in 23 hours 20 minutes, and I was so proud.

That last 18 kilometres was one of the hardest things I have ever done. With hindsight I was probably too confident at the 50, and then I went too fast. I was ignoring my heartbeat monitor, and didn't stick to what I'd planned.

But I now recognise the value of committing to an 'Awesome and Ridiculous Goal!'

Summary

Always strive for something more out of life. When you accomplish a goal, make a new one. Nothing is impossible, because where there is a will, there is a way. It doesn't matter if you want to build a multi-billion pound industry, or whether you want to go bungee jumping - make a plan and make it happen!

Never get bored. If you find yourself getting bored, it's time to move on and find new things to do. Boredom is the killer of motivation and energy; the drain of your life force.

Make or review your Bucket List. Cross off things you've accomplished. Notice what's stopping you or holding you back from the things you haven't done, and do something about them. Add a few new things for good measure. BIG ones. Oh, and don't be a CANT. Have I mentioned that?

Next steps

1. ☐

2. ☐

3. ☐

Chapter 8
It's great to be in the zone

"I've missed more than 9000 shots in my career, I've lost almost 300 games. 26 times, I've been trusted to take the game winning shot and missed. I've failed over and over and over again in my life. And that is why I succeed."
Michael Jordan

"People tend to play in their comfort zone, so the best things are achieved in a state of surprise, actually."
Brian Eno

Staying in 'The Zone' takes a lot of time and effort. It's a fantastic, timeless place. So how exactly do you get there?

In The Zone, you can think clearly and meet challenges with skill and ease. It's that place where you just know that you can't put a foot wrong - where you're confident, capable, calm and collected. How useful is that?

Move Zone

Most people will stay safe in their Comfort Zone most of the time; they're on snooze mode. When the heat is turned on and they start to experience difficulty and/or challenge, they flip up into the Panic Zone. If they can cope with that (and want to progress), they can move into the Learning Zone where they can develop skills, experience and abilities to cope with the challenge. But for most people, it's a very easy ride back down in to the Comfort Zone once the challenge is past.

Sometimes life blindsides you, and you get thrown into the Panic Zone. The trick is to learn from those challenges, not be defeated by them. In time, you'll be

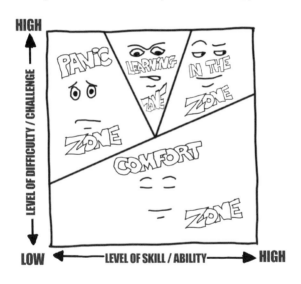

able to cross straight from the Comfort Zone into The Zone when confronted by a challenge, or to move directly from the Panic Zone into it. Because The Zone is where it all happens. The Zone is where you truly CAN. If you're in the Panic Zone, you're much more likely to act like a CANT.

Houston, we have a problem...

When I watched that wonderful movie 'Apollo 13', I realised it's an extraordinary example of being in 'The Zone' or in 'Flow' - and in the most trying of circumstances; a real matter of life or death.

I was a young boy at the time of the Apollo 13 mission, and I can remember the excitement and fear when the accident happened, the anxiety for the days it took for Apollo 13 to return, and the pure joy and elation when it splashed down safely and the 3 astronauts emerged from their spaceship.

Apollo 13 launched on 11th April 1970. It was the third Apollo flight scheduled to land on the Moon, with a crew of Commander Jim Lovell, Jack Swiggert and Fred Haise. It was comprised of 3 modules: a command module (where the crew spent most of their time as it journeyed through space), a service module (which housed the power and life support systems) and the lunar module. This lunar module was deployed once the command module was orbiting the moon, so Lovell and Haise could land and then return to the command module, which would then leave moon's orbit and return to Earth. Good plan, but…

It was an uneventful journey (Comfort Zone) until on 13th April, Mission Control in Houston asked Swiggert to turn on the hydrogen and oxygen tank stirring fans. A few seconds later, one of the oxygen cylinders exploded, knocking out all the command module's power and life services (Panic Zone)! It was then that the famous message was radioed: "Houston, we have a problem."

Apollo astronauts were the crème de la crème and trained for most eventualities (Learning Zone), but nobody ever predicted this. Their only chance of survival was to abandon the command module, move into the tiny lunar module and live off of its independent power and life support systems. The decision was taken in an instant.

In effect, they had a life boat. The plan from there was to travel to the moon, slingshot around it and back to Earth. Houston Control was constantly feeding them data and new procedures, to minimise power usage and get the re-entry trajectory correct.

If ever there was an example of being in The Zone, of being in 'Flow', this was it, especially for Captain Jim Lovell. Despite all of the challenges he faced he remained calm and focussed at all times. The movie is well worth another watch.

Summary

It's all too easy to stay in our comfort zone, and only come out when we're pushed out and into panic. Then it's even easier to drop back into comfort when the panic's over. Use the panic as an impetus to shift you into the learning zone, to get the most learning from any situation.

Being in 'The Zone' is a wonderful experience, and I try to get into it (and stay there) as often as I can. Once experienced, you'll want to, too!

Next steps

1. ☐

2. ☐

3. ☐

Chapter 9
Steal from the best and leave the rest

"It is not our abilities that show what we truly are. It is our choices." **Dumbledore (aka J K Rowling)**

"Good artists copy. Great artists steal." **Pablo Picasso**

If you don't have what you need, then do the research, read up and immerse yourself in the Learning Zone.

Acquire Skills by Stealing, Borrowing or Buying Them

Not having the skills you need to get the job done is no excuse for giving up. If you're not talented in that way, you have a few options.

Option 1: Steal what you need. I do accept that morally, it's not ideal. But it gets you what you need, and as long as nobody is harmed... I would never advocate ripping off someone's work, for example stealing art, music etc. But why reinvent the wheel when you can nick one off someone else and reverse engineer it to make your own? You can STEAL. Find someone knowledgeable, and suck them dry of all the information you need.

Option 2: Borrow the skills or knowledge you need. Have someone lend you what you need to do the job, or BORROW one of their staff who can do it.

Option 3: Buy. Accept that you don't have what you need, and, more to the point, it's a waste of your time and energy to get it. So BUY in what you need. We all do this, almost on a daily basis. Do you service your own car? Plumb in a new shower? Pave your own drive? Unlikely. You buy those skills in - remember the phrase 'the hired help'?

For more complex needs such as programming, marketing, webpages, writing, etc, the Internet is full of freelance marketplaces where you can list the project you need help with, and get quotes from several different people. Best of all, these systems protect both you and the freelancer you hire, so you don't have to worry about wasting the money and getting something that you don't want or can't use.

The point is, if you need the skills, don't be a CANT about it.

Sometimes Knowing is Better Than No-No-ing

I can't tell you how much money I've lost over the years on various ventures. I'll get what seems like a good idea (at the time) in my head, and once I've got hold of it I'm tenacious and never like to give up. Possibly because I am OCF (Obsessive, Compulsive, Focussed ☺). So I often spend loads of time and money on a bright idea of mine and I might even go through with it, when I could have just asked somebody for an opinion, or gone to the best in that field and got advice that would have saved myself an awful lot of money.

For instance, I found a drink in Thailand called 'Hang' that I thought was a fantastic product. It's supposed to prevent hangovers. So of course, I had to personally carry out some rigorous product testing, which I did with a mate. We got this bottle of 'Hang', downed it about 8 o'clock at night, and got absolutely rat-arsed. We drank, we mixed our drinks, we did everything we could think of and a few things we don't remember. In the morning we got up, had breakfast and felt fine, and we were a bit baffled. We should be feeling like death - what was going on? Then we remembered the 'Hang'...

Now I knew this was a fantastic product! But being thorough, just to prove the experiment wasn't a fluke, we did exactly the same the next night - and lo and behold, it worked again. I thought I had my hands on liquid gold. I had to ship this to the U.K.

Instead of just importing a load of stuff and then learning about the drinks business, I asked myself who I knew; who was my best contact in this area. I happened to know Gordon Bromley, the former Managing Director of Tropicana UK who had taken Tropicana from nothing to about £150 million a year in this country. So if anybody knew how to distribute a drink, he was my man - and not only that, but maybe I could get him on board and use his expertise and do the venture together. He knew me well, and he knew that I get enthusiastic about something and I want to spend money on it, learning about the business and moving forward - whether I have the advice or not.

So I talked to him about it, and he went pretty pale, which I thought was a bit odd. So I asked him, "Why such a long face? This thing's going to be huge!" He told me, "It could be huge, probably should be, but you're up against some big global mega brands who won't want you in the market. I'd be really excited if it weren't so hard; and here's why…"

He told me that in 2006 when he was at the top of his game, he was closely involved in the launch of a product called 'TAUT'. It was an amazing sports drink that knocked the brand leaders, Lucozade™ (owned by Glaxo Smith Kline™), Powerade™ (The Coca Cola Company) and Gatorade (PepsiCo) right out of the park on quality. It had fantastic differentiation and USP's, good funding and, after successful regional testing, all the top retailers had listed it nationally. Success seemed assured, but then, all of a sudden, they started hitting snags.

Mysterious rumours started circulating about impurities in the product and anonymous "consumer" letters were sent in their hundreds to retailers and trade press questioning the clinical performance trials. Retailer promotion slots jumped overnight from £3000 to £10,000 a time and product mysteriously disappeared from in-store shelves despite good stockholding. It was all nonsense, but the issues kept coming and soon management were spending more time fighting smoke and mirrors than running the business. Not surprisingly, the funding and the energy eventually ran out and a wonderful new product was forced out of the market.

I wanted to get Gordon involved and use his expertise (STEAL), because I didn't want to spend all the time necessary learning about the industry. But he gave me the advice I needed to make my decision about 'Hang', for which I'm grateful, as it has saved me a lot of time and money.

I'd like to use this anecdote to illustrate several things - and this can apply to your own organisation or situation, not just to this specific situation. CANTS can close you down. CANTS can steal your energy. CANS recognise the value of needed advice (be it bought, borrowed or stolen). Thanks to Gordon and AICIRI, I KNEW that 'Hang' wasn't going to fly in the UK after all. CANS move on from defeat. I crossed the bridge. I didn't look back. CANS don't cry over spilt milk.

Summary

You can get anywhere you want; you just need a little help from time to time. If you don't have what you need, steal, borrow, or buy it. Ask an expert. Do your own research. Hire someone who knows and can do what you need. Just get it done and dusted, so you can focus on the things that you are good at.

Once you commit to the impossible, it's not so impossible anymore. You just have to set your mind to it. Develop a strategy, and then GET IT DONE.

You've reached the end of this book. But don't let that stop you. Here's some free advice - read this book again! The more you think about what's in here, the more likely you are to absorb and adopt what it has to offer. This book is, by its very nature, highly contextual. You'll want to apply its lessons to the content of your own life. Re-reading this will help you earn and own this knowledge.

So, for now it's over to you. Review your notes and get to work! Be lucky, and be happy. You have the responsibility to make yourself happy, but I have helped, and now leave you a little more (or even a lot more) beautiful than you were before. I've even helpfully filled in your first next step for you. ☺

Next steps

1. Read this book again! ☺   ☐

2.   ☐

3.   ☐

Summary

RULE AND TOOL SUMMARY SYNOPSIS
(Easy to remember)

GET THE ESSENCE - YOU CAN
get the best out of this life.

Chapter 1 What's the point? Get CONTEXT in your life.

Chapter 2 WHY do this? Have a purpose to your life.

Chapter 3 Less is more? Be effective in your life.

GET THE ENERGY - YOU CAN
get the energy you need out of this life.

Chapter 4 Stay off the triangle.

Chapter 5 Balance and Alignment in your world.

Chapter 6 Let's talk about spilt milk and crossed bridges.

GET THE IMPOSSIBLE - YOU CAN
get what you want from this life

Chapter 7 Do terrifying and exciting stuff.

Chapter 8 It's great to be in the zone.

Chapter 9 Steal from the best and leave the rest.

If you want a few NEXT STEPS to try out the Essence of this book, try these:

Live your life in accordance with Rudyard Kipling's poem 'If'.

Create a world like John Lennon describes in 'Imagine'.

Oh and one last thing...

Try to be nicer to each other.

Frank's biography

Frank is a successful businessman with a beating, happy heart.

As CEO of Bastows, London's premier property restoration and redecoration company, Frank leads a team of dedicated professionals committed to 'Making London Beautiful'. His other business interests currently include an Accounting Practice with a different approach to Industry, an HR and Wellbeing Consultancy business and a Software Testing Company, along with many other start-ups he has had the privilege to help.

Frank has a passion for coaching start-up entrepreneurs, helping them to find focus in their new adventure and to understand their true purpose. In simple terms, he drives context, manages energy and coaches the skills required to enable both businesses and individuals to thrive and survive on their own.

Frank combines experience in sales, accountancy and performing expertise, a wonderful mix that he uses to enhance his naturally charismatic and enthusiastic approach to everything he gets involved in.

A commitment to leading by example, unwavering honesty and a deep spirit of fairness underpin the success of all Frank's businesses, benefiting clients, employees and colleagues alike. He wants to share his energy and enthusiasm, and loves to enable others to discover their own intents and contexts, which will in turn facilitate positive change for them, their businesses and everyone involved.

Frank is married to Amanda and lives in Surrey with their 4 children, aged between 11 and 23.

He is a keen poker player. This hobby seems to have stuck around longer than his normal infatuations, as he still believes he can be world champion one day soon.

This is his current Awesome & Ridiculous Goal at the time of writing this book.

Our sources and suggested further places to explore

"More Money, More Time, Less Stress", The business owner's guide to creating a profitable, sustainable business that rewards you richly in time and money - John Rosling, Shirlaws.

Frameworks used: CONTEXT: SOURCE OUTCOME: INTENT: THINK FEEL KNOW: POSITIONING

"How to Win Friends and Influence People" - Dale Carnegie

"How to Stop Worrying and Start Living" - Dale Carnegie

"How to be a Complete and Utter Failure" - Steve McDermott, (Audio CD)

"Unlimited Power - The New Science of Personal Achievement" - Anthony Robbins

"The Magic of Thinking Big" - David J. Schwartz

"Think and Grow Rich" - Napoleon Hill

"Start with Why", - Simon Sinek,
"Effortless Success: How to Get What You Want and Have a Great Time Doing It!" - Michael Neill, - (Audio CD)

"Flow: The Psychology of Happiness: The Classic Work on How to Achieve Happiness" - Mihaly Csikszentmihalyi and Csikszentmihaly

"The Art of War" - Sun Tzu

And finally . . . .

A very special thanks to Shirlaws for allowing us to beg, steal and borrow some of their ideas, and to **Darren Shirlaw** for inventing it all in the first place!

No he didn't! Well, not all of it! As I said before, everyone begs, steals or borrows…

EUREKA MOMENTS
(Write your Next Steps and Ideas here)

1. Recommend this book to everyone you know & care about ☺ ☐

2. ☐

3. ☐

4. ☐

5. ☐

6. ☐

7. ☐

8. ☐

9. ☐

10. ☐

This edition published January 2014 in the United Kingdom by:
YesWeCan Publishing
12-14 Bridge Street
Leatherhead
Surrey KT22 8BZ

A CIP record of this book is available from the British Library.

Printed in the UK by Halstan

Layout and design by David W Watts
www.dwwdesign.com

ISBN 978-1-78280-222-8